Animal Homes

Spiders and Their Webs

Argiope garden spider

by Linda Tagliaferro

Consulting Editor: Gail Saunders-Smith, Ph.D.

Consultant: Jeremy Miller, Ph.D.
Department of Systematic Biology–Entomology
National Museum of Natural History
Smithsonian Institution, Washington, D.C.

Capstone
press

Mankato, Minnesota

Pebble Plus is published by Capstone Press,
151 Good Counsel Drive, P.O. Box 669, Mankato, Minnesota 56002.
www.capstonepress.com

1 2 3 4 5 6 09 08 07 06 05 04

Library of Congress Cataloging-in-Publication Data
Tagliaferro, Linda.
Spiders and their webs / by Linda Tagliaferro.
    p. cm.—(Pebble Plus, animal homes)
    Includes bibliographical references and index.
    ISBN-13: 978-0-7368-2385-2 (hardcover)
    ISBN-10: 0-7368-2385-9 (hardcover)
    ISBN-13: 978-0-7368-5125-1 (softcover pbk.)
    ISBN-10: 0-7368-5125-9 (softcover pbk.)
    1. Spiders—Juvenile literature. 2. Spider webs—Juvenile literature. I. Title. II. Series:
    Pebble Plus, animal homes (Mankato, Minn.)
QL458.4.T34 2004
595.4′4—dc22   2003013428

Summary: Simple text and photographs describe spiders and their webs.

Editorial Credits
Martha E. H. Rustad, editor; Linda Clavel, series designer; Deirdre Barton and Wanda Winch,
    photo researchers; Karen Risch, product planning editor

Photo Credits
Bill Johnson, 10–11
Bruce Coleman Inc./Gail M. Shumway, 6–7; Ivan Polunin, 19
Corbis/Craig Tuttle, cover
Minden Pictures/Gerry Ellis, 13, 16–17; Konrad Wothe, 5, 20–21; Mark Moffett, 14–15
Photodisc, Inc./Geostock, 1
Unicorn Stock Photos/Ron Partis, 9

Pebble Plus thanks Gary Dunn, director of education at the Young Entomologists' Society in Lansing, Michigan, for his assistance with this book.

Note to Parents and Teachers

The Animal Homes series supports national science standards related to life science. This book describes and illustrates spiders and their webs. The images support early readers in understanding the text. The repetition of words and phrases helps early readers learn new words. This book also introduces early readers to subject-specific vocabulary words, which are defined in the Glossary. Early readers may need assistance to read some words and to use the Table of Contents, Glossary, Read More, Internet Sites, and Index/Word List sections of the book.

Word Count: 187
Early-Intervention Level: 17

Table of Contents

Webs

Spiders build webs on
plants, rocks, and buildings.
Spiders are arachnids.
They have eight legs and
two body sections.

orb-weaving spider ➡

5

Spiders build webs with strings of silk. Spiders make silk in their bodies.

black widow spider ➡

Some spiders weave webs in circles. Some spiders weave webs in flat sheets. Some spiders weave webs with silk strings in all directions. Some spiders do not build webs.

orb web ➡

9

Some spiders live in the same web for a long time. Some spiders make new webs every day. These spiders work for about one hour to build a web.

funnelweb spider ➤

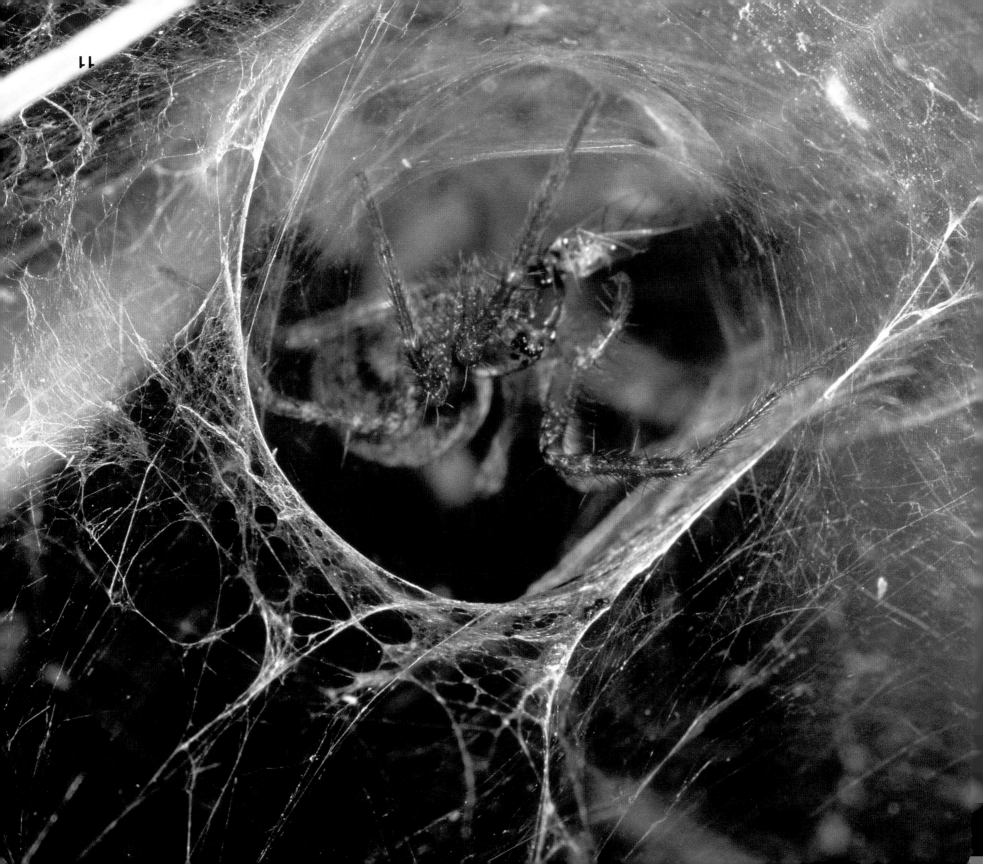

◄ orb-weaving spider

Catching Insects

Spiders catch insects to eat.
The sticky webs trap insects.
Spiders do not stick to their
own webs.

Egg Sacs

Female spiders also use silk to make egg sacs. They lay eggs in the egg sacs. Some spiders lay two eggs. Others lay 1,000 eggs.

tarantula eggs ➡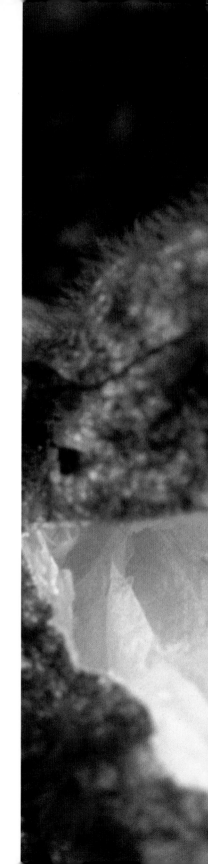

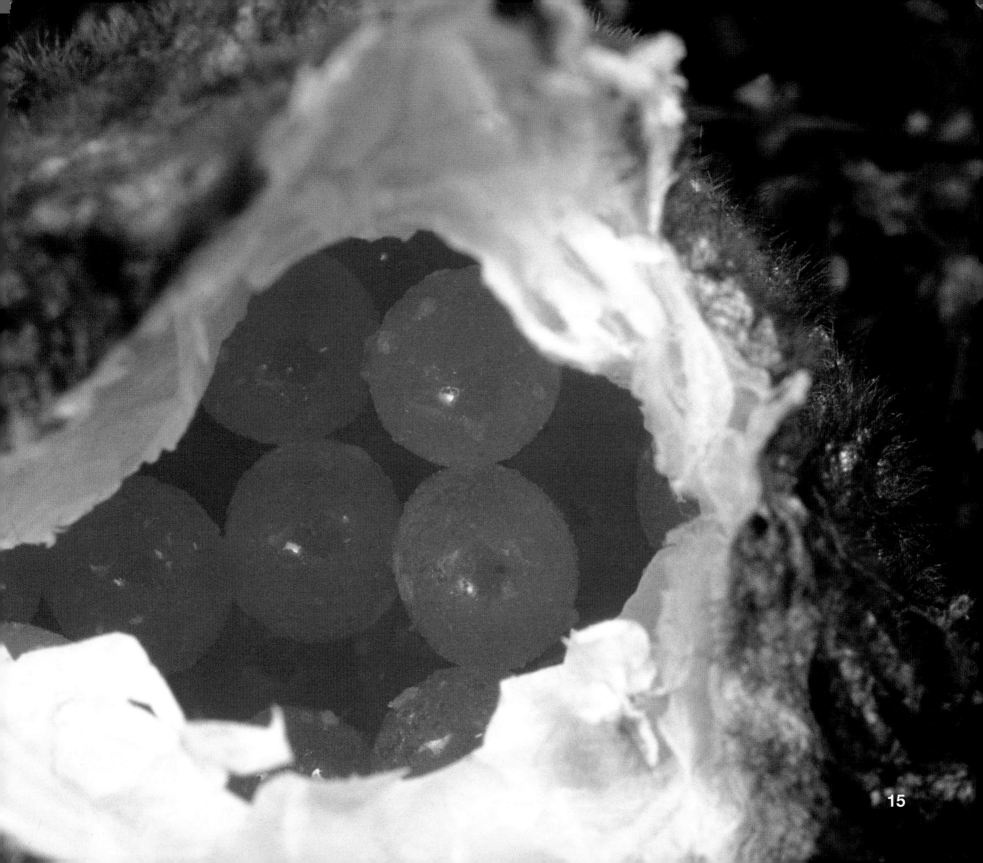

Spiders carry or hide
their silk egg sacs.
Hungry animals cannot
find the egg sacs.

huntsman spider ➤

Spiderlings hatch from the egg sac. Spiderlings use silk to float through the air. Spiderlings find a new place to build their own webs.

spiderlings ➡

A Good Home

Different kinds of spiders
build different kinds of webs.
No two webs are the same.

funnelweb spider ➡

Glossary

arachnid—a small animal with eight legs, two main body sections, and a hard outer shell

egg sac—a small holder for eggs; spiders make the egg sac from silk; each egg sac can hold up to 1,000 eggs.

insect—a small animal with six legs, three main body sections, and a hard outer shell; most insects have two or four wings.

silk—a string made by spiders; spiders use silk to build webs, homes, and egg sacs.

spiderling—a young spider

weave—to put strings together; spiders weave silk strings into webs.

Read More

Pascoe, Elaine. *Spiders Spin Silk.* How & Why. Milwaukee: Gareth Stevens, 2002.

Squire, Ann O. *Spiders.* A True Book. New York: Children's Press, 2003.

Stefoff, Rebecca. *Spider.* Living Things. New York: Benchmark Books, 1999.

Internet Sites

FactHound offers a safe, fun way to find Internet sites related to this book. All of the sites on FactHound have been researched by our staff.

Here's how:

1. Visit *www.facthound.com*

2. Type in this special code **0736823859** for age-appropriate sites. Or enter a search word related to this book for a more general search.

3. Click on the **Fetch It** button.

FactHound will fetch the best sites for you!

Index/Word List